You Are A
Liberal Deux

You Are A
Liberal Deux

John M. Bushman, III

gatekeeper press

Columbus, Ohio

You Are A Liberal Deux

Published by Gatekeeper Press

2167 Stringtown Rd, Suite 109

Columbus, OH 43123-2989

www.GatekeeperPress.com

The cover design, interior formatting, typesetting, and editorial work for this book are entirely the product of the author. Gatekeeper Press did not participate in and is not responsible for any aspect of these elements.

ISBN (paperback): 9781662900969

Dedication

To all the people that voted
to take our country back by electing
Donald Trump as President.

Forward

This book gives you an in-depth look into the mind of a liberal. You would be wise in sharing this book with a few of your friends and family members. Regardless, if you are a liberal, independent, or a conservative, we can all benefit from this book.

Jesus said you shall know the truth and the truth shall make you free. After reading this book, I promise you will be set free from liberal bondage. This book will not only inform the reader but will also transform the mindset and lifestyle of the reader.

I am a black man, a Christian man and a conservative man. I am constantly berated because I refuse to think and live like a liberal. President Donald J. Trump was chosen by God and elected by the American people. President Trump is Pro God, Pro Israel, Pro Life and Pro America. President Trump desires for all of us to win and win some more. Refusing to believe any of what has been stated, clearly indicates you are a liberal.

My name is Apostle DJ Wiggins
and I am a TRUMPfighter.

You are a liberal if you think Russia was able to influence the outcome of the American Election.

You are a liberal if your candidate lost, but not because the other candidate was a better option.

You are a liberal if you don't believe in right and wrong because everything is relative.

You are a liberal if you think George W. Bush stole the election in 2000 and 2004.

The Answer is :
TRUMPtastic - The American People,
Making America Great.

You are a liberal if you don't believe in black and white but only in grays.

You are a liberal if you think compassion is getting more people enrolled in government programs.

You are a liberal if you suspect the entire Republican party is run by the pro-life movement.

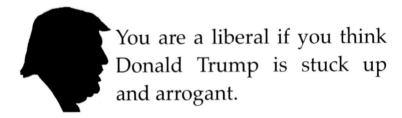 You are a liberal if you think Donald Trump is stuck up and arrogant.

You are a liberal if you believe that Rush Limbaugh is an elitist.

The Answer is:
TRUMPster - Anyone that benefits from the policies of the Trump administration.

You are a liberal if you think that Fox News Network is conservative.

You are a liberal if you believe that Donald Trump is destroying America.

You are a liberal if you think ABC, CBS, NBC and all cable channels report the truth.

You are a liberal if you think the 65 million folks that voted for Hillary Clinton are the mainstream of the American people.

You are a liberal if you believe that Michael Moore is a great filmmaker.

The Answer is:
TRUMPnado - A whirlwind of great economic news sweeping over the whole nation.

You are a liberal if you think that children are being taken away from parents by Donald Trump.

You are a liberal if you think gay marriages should be considered normal.

You are a liberal if you believe that elitists are the best at running the government.

You are a liberal if you live in a blue county and think that your county reflects the entire country.

You are a liberal if you want everybody to "just get along."

The Answer is:
unTRUMPable - The American people standing up to the establishment and electing a president for the good of the country.

You are a liberal if you believe the Occupy Movement is a peaceful demonstration against social and economic inequality.

You are a liberal if you think the term social justice is all about helping people in need.

You are a liberal if you think using the term terrorists will make them feel bad or hurt their feelings.

You are a liberal if you think everyone needs to pay more in taxes.

The Answer is:
TRUMPolicious - Joy waking up everyday knowing Donald Trump is the president.

You are a liberal if you want and believe in big government.

You are a liberal if you believe everyone else is having a hard time making a living.

You are a liberal if you lie to get on a talk radio station.

You are a liberal if you think George Bush went to war in Iraq because of oil.

You are a liberal if you exempt yourself from the laws that others must obey.

The Answer is:
TRUMPeter - Someone that sounds the alarm and provides solution to liberal problems.

 You are a liberal if you think the constitution dictates the separation of Church and State.

You are a liberal if only establishment people should be the candidate of your party.

You are a liberal if you want to leave this country because the president is a Republican.

You are a liberal if you think a decrease in the rate of growth for government programs is a budget cut.

You are a liberal if you think that Republicans lie.

The Answer is:
TRUMPology - The words and policies that make up the Trump Agenda.

You are a liberal if you use illegal drugs and think they are beneficial.

You are a liberal if you said that Bill Clinton was like the first black president of the country.

You are a liberal if you believe that life begins with the first breath.

You are a liberal if you think Sean Hannity is not a great American.

You are a liberal if you think that the military is occupying other countries.

The Answer is:
TRUMPography - Any pictures of President Trump surrounded by the HUGE crowds when he speaks.

 You are a liberal if you believe that Israel is occupying the West Bank.

You are a liberal if you think black helicopters are flying by your house at night.

You are a liberal if you think that Saddam Hussein and Osama Bin Laden knew each other.

You are a liberal if you think Ronald Reagan and Donald Trump are evil men.

You are a liberal if you think a business owner views his employees as slaves.

The Answer is:
TRUMPfire - The roar of excitement as the Trump economy spreads through America.

You are a liberal if you believe the minimum wage is too low.

You are a liberal if you think that the United States Armed Services are not needed.

You are a liberal if you think that the United Nations should have more power.

You are a liberal if the US military costs too much money.

 You are a liberal if you're a RINO (Republican In Name Only).

The Answer is:
TRUMPortunity - The way of creating a favorable environment for people to prosper.

You are a liberal if you ask voters to support the establishment candidate, but when the party picks a person that isn't an establishment candidate you don't support the pick of the party.

You are a liberal if you want someone like Mikhail Gorbachev or Vladimir Putin to bring back the U.S.S.R.

You are a liberal if you think the United States has too much power.

You are a liberal if you think the winners should listen to the losers.

The Answer is:
TRUMPexpectancy - Realizing that each day Donald Trump is in office as president, America keeps on improving.

 You are a liberal if you don't think that the United States of America is the best country ever.

You are a liberal if you believe in man made climate change.

You are a liberal if you are confused.

You are a liberal if you think Donald Trump is racist.

You are a liberal if you think the rich aren't paying enough taxes.

You are a liberal if you like unions.

The Answer is:
TRUMPville - A community where people want to help their fellow neighbors.

You are a liberal if you keep doing the same thing over and over again, expecting different results.

You are a liberal if you think communism still hasn't had a chance to prove itself.

You are a liberal if you think Donald Trump doesn't keep his promises.

You are a liberal if you believe a tax cut takes money away from the government.

You are a liberal if you think Donald Trump is like Hitler.

The Answer is:
TRUMPerica - A place where "truth, justice and the American way" are found.

You are a liberal if you consider someone earning $35,000 a year rich.

You are a liberal if you want a refund after buying this book.

You are a liberal if you value the environment more than people.

You are a liberal if you think that you can change the world by becoming a journalist.

You are a liberal if you believe that freedom comes from the press.

The Answer is:
TRUMPromoter - Those that see the good President Trump is doing and let others know.

You are a liberal if you think people should believe the way you do. (Rush Limbaugh is exempt).

You are a liberal if you think the constitution is a living, breathing document.

You are a liberal if you don't think Donald Trump is popular.

You are a liberal if you think there are fewer trees today, than last year.

You are a liberal if you have stopped reading this book.

The Answer is:
TRUMPower - The president empowering citizens to achieve their dreams.

You are a liberal if your are not laughing at the comments made in this book.

You are a liberal if you don't like this book.

You are a liberal if you think that dolphins are smarter than people.

You are a liberal if you are mad at this book.

You are a liberal if you don't want books like this published.

You are a liberal if you're trying to find contradictions in this book.

The Answer is:
TRUMPatience - Standing firm while the establishment takes their best shot over and over again.

You are a liberal if you say you have an open mind, but don't want to listen to other viewpoints.

You are a liberal if you want to choose the middle of the road and not pick a side.

 You are a liberal if you think $2 + 2 = 5$.

You are a liberal if you think calling yourself a progressive will make people think you are not a liberal.

You are a liberal if you think that water and air are dirtier because of Republicans.

The Answer is:
TRUMPchosen - The leader of the Free World.

You are a liberal if you think there is nothing good about Republican presidents.

 You are a liberal if you think Hollywood is the mainstream of America.

You are a liberal if you think more animals need to be added to the endangered list.

You are a liberal if you think the endangered animal list is getting shorter.

You are a liberal if you believe that human beings are destroying the planet Earth.

The Answer is:
TRUMPgration - Larger numbers of Hispanics, African Americans and women voting for Donald Trump over other Republicans in recent years.

You are a liberal if you think the universe is being destroyed by people.

You are a liberal if you think people are the cause for the hole in the ozone layer.

You are a liberal if you have all the answers.

You are a liberal if you think judges should be activists making decisions based on opinions.

You are a liberal if you think you are better than anyone else.

The Answer is:
TRUMPnation - Thanks to the
founding fathers for putting in place
the electoral college.

You are a liberal if you think we have a deficit because the president is spending the money.

You are a liberal if you think there is too much money in politics.

You are a liberal if you think public education needs more money.

You are a liberal if you enjoy spending other people's money.

You are a liberal if you believe only a limited amount of money is available.

The Answer is:
TRUMPromise - Doing exactly what
he said he would do.

You are a liberal if you think convicted felons should have the right to vote.

You are a liberal if you believe the underdog needs your help to survive.

You are a liberal if you think Donald Trump is stupid.

 You are a liberal if you think the EU are friends of the United States.

You are a liberal if you want the country to fail in order to get rid of Donald Trump.

You are a liberal if you are a moderate.

The Answer is:
TRUMPday - Another day the Trump card has been played against the establishment.

You are a liberal if you think a tax refund on April 15th is a way of cheating the government.

You are a liberal if you want something for free that you have the ability to pay for.

You are a liberal if you think we are a divided country.

You are a liberal if you believe the country is broken because of a Republican president.

You are a liberal if you think the president is supposed to do things for you.

The Answer is:
TRUMPoetry - Donald Trump
making America jump for joy.

You are a liberal if you think Justice Clarence Thomas is really white.

You are a liberal if a Democrat president can do nothing wrong.

You are a liberal if you don't want to Make America Great Again.

 You are a liberal if you think we need more laws against guns.

You are a liberal if you think Republicans cheat.

You are a liberal if you think people that live in the Red States are idiots.

The Answer is:
TRUMPgenious - The world leaders seeking the United States and Donald Trump because their country will benefit being friends.

You are a liberal if you feel sorry for homeless people who have options.

You are a liberal if you like to see soup kitchen lines.

You are a liberal if you think homelessness happens only when Republicans are in office.

You are a liberal if you think Donald Trump became president for selfish reasons.

You are a liberal if you think Republicans use voter fraud.

The Answer is:
TRUMPmazing - Drawing crowds
like a rock star.

You are a liberal if you think that you are worse off financially when a Republican is president.

You are a liberal if you believe that evolution is scientific and has nothing to do with faith.

You are a liberal if you think there are more rich Republicans then rich Democrats.

 You are a liberal if you think zoos are cruel places for animals.

You are a liberal if you are a PBS contributor.

The Answer is:
TRUMPgiant - Taking on all challengers and coming out on top.

You are a liberal if you think marriage is bondage.

You are a liberal if you want Camelot back.

You are a liberal (elitist) if you value style over substance.

You are a liberal if character doesn't matter.

You are a liberal if the seriousness of the charge is enough to start an investigation.

You are a liberal if you don't like using the term welfare program and prefer to call it EBT because it's less offensive.

The Answer is:
TRUMPboom - income up,
unemployment down, stock market
up, bankruptcies down.

You are a liberal if you take our freedom for granted.

You are a liberal if you think that America is a selfish nation.

 You are a liberal if you think America is a bully.

You are a liberal if you think America wants to control the world.

You are a liberal if you think Donald Trump doesn't care for America.

You are a liberal if you want old people put out of their misery.

The Answer is:
TRUMPanator - Liberals acting confused and in decline.

You are a liberal if Republicans getting elected has nothing to do with morality.

You are a liberal if you think Donald Trump doesn't like you.

You are a liberal if the Ten Commandments offend you.

You are a liberal if you think the Ten Commandments are a Charlton Heston Movie.

You are a liberal if you think school vouchers would destroy public education.

The Answer is:
TRUMPluminous - A bright future
for America.

You are a liberal if you think that kooks are in the Republican party.

You are a liberal if you think the flag should be burned instead of flown.

You are a liberal if you feel guilty because you live in America.

You are a liberal if you think war never works.

You are a liberal if you live your life with a September 10th, 2001 mentality.

You are a liberal if you want more laws put in place to limit others' freedoms.

The Answer is:
TRUMPeace - People everywhere enjoying life.

You are a liberal if you want revenge.

You are a liberal if you think that people that believe in creation are ignorant.

You are a liberal if you act conservative to get elected.

You are a liberal if you don't understand when Donald Trump is telling a joke.

You are a liberal if you act conservative when talking to certain people.

You are a liberal if you are a sexist.

You are a liberal if you generalize.

The Answer is:
TRUMPlanet - World leaders
looking to Trump for answers.

You are a liberal if you will do or say anything to get elected.

You are a liberal if you feel you have to tell people how great you are.

You are a liberal if you think welfare is a great government program.

 You are a liberal if you think more people on food stamps is a success.

You are a liberal if you say one thing and do the opposite.

You are a liberal if you believe in outcome based education.

The Answer is:
TRUMPuniverse - The cosmos
realigning and becoming great.

You are a liberal if you think competition is bad.

You are a liberal if you think monopolies are bad.

You are a liberal if you don't have core values.

 You are a liberal if you don't want to Keep America Great.

You are a liberal if you think capitalism is bad.

You are a liberal if you think communism is good.

The Answer is:
TRUMPstar - More than just a location on the Hollywood Walk of Fame.

 You are a liberal if you think Christians want to impose their beliefs on you.

You are a liberal if you laugh at televangelists.

You are a liberal if you think Israel is the problem.

You are a liberal if you think the world is overpopulated.

You are a liberal if you think that the public library is full of good books.

You are a liberal if you think animals are nice to each other.

The Answer is:
TRUMPboss - A businessman,
running this country like a well
oiled machine.

You are a liberal if you think people need to learn how to behave from animals.

You are a liberal if you think animals are not a food source.

You are a liberal if you think in general that people are mean.

You are a liberal if you promote victims.

CAUTION
DON'T
BE A
VICTIM

You are a liberal if you don't think we need a wall on our borders.

You are a liberal if you think that truth is something nobody can know.

You are a liberal if you like discord.

The Answer is:
TRUMPleader - The most powerful
man in the world.

You are a liberal if you think that people don't understand your ideas.

You are a liberal if you think trees are only to be looked at.

 You are a liberal if you think trees are not to be used to make paper or wood.

You are a liberal if you think everyone should eat only what you eat.

You are a liberal if you think sex education needs to be taught in school.

You are a liberal if you think schools are better parents than moms and dads.

The Answer is:
TRUMPking - Ruling over the political establishment in Washington DC and wherever they are found.

You are a liberal if you think men are dictators.

You are a liberal if you think women are not in control.

You are a liberal if you think your friends need you and that they can't make it without you.

 You are a liberal if you don't want to offend anybody.

You are a liberal if you want everybody to like you.

You are a liberal if you are concerned about hurting anyone's feelings.

The Answer is:
TRUMPism - Teacher, like a rabbi, supreme, leader, Trump having a strong bond with the voters.

You are a liberal if you care what people think about you.

 You are a liberal if you think people like you because of how you look.

You are a liberal if you do things for people because you want something.

You are a liberal if you feel sorry for other people groups.

You are a liberal if you think that SUV's are living machines that have no use for a driver and when in the news they appear to control themselves.

You are a liberal if you are a racist.

The Answer is:
TRUMPlove - Trust between
President Trump and the American
people.

You are a liberal if the cross offends you.

You are a liberal if the Bible offends you.

You are a liberal if Christians offend you.

You are a liberal if you think that Jesus is a brainwasher or used as a crutch.

You are a liberal if you think Rush Limbaugh is arrogant.

You are a liberal if you think it is OK to cheat on your taxes.

You are a liberal if you think that non-profit organizations are crooked.

The Answer is:
TRUMPremium - The best, perfect, outstanding, prime option for president.

You are a liberal if you think you don't have to give to the needy because you are sure others are giving.

You are a liberal if you think you are a better person because you care more than others.

You are a liberal if you think Republicans are sexists, racists, bigots, and homophobes.

You are a liberal if you laugh when bad things happen to others.

You are a liberal if you think Republicans are angry white men.

The Answer is:
TRUMPtrain - Jump on board for the most exciting ride of our lives.

You are a liberal if it's OK for Democrats to raise money in churches but not Republicans.

You are a liberal if you think the Pledge of Allegiance needs the  phrase "One Nation under God" taken out.

 You are a liberal if you think that the phrase "In God we Trust" needs to be taken off our currency.

You are a liberal if you think Newt Gingrich had a contract on America.

You are a liberal if you are a homophobe.

> The Answer is:
> TRUMPsmart - Knowing how to respond to all the liberal lies.

You are a liberal if you think televangelists are con artists.

 You are a liberal if you think people like you because you have the right car or house.

You are a liberal if you think that Zell Miller is a traitor.

You are a liberal if you want to see others suffer so you can continue to benefit from them.

You are a liberal if you think the outcome of the Washington Redskins football game in an election year predicts the outcome.

The Answer is:
TRUMPtruth - Elected 45th
president by the people of the
United States.

You are a liberal if you think that illegal aliens deserve all the rights that legal residents get.

You are a liberal if you think Pat Robertson talks with Donald Trump everyday.

 You are a liberal if you think your candidate won the debate because they had a better hair style.

You are a liberal if you think the Republican National Committee talks with Rush Limbaugh everyday.

You are a liberal if you think the axis of evil is a geometry problem gone bad.

The Answer is:
TRUMPjustice - Preserve, protect and defend the Constitution of the United States and upholding the laws in force.

You are a liberal if you think natural disasters are no longer natural.

You are a liberal if you think that your fellow veterans are liars because they are Republicans.

You are a liberal if you think your candidate won the debate because they had a better suntan.

You are a liberal if you're more comfortable in Canada than in the USA.

You are a liberal if you can't describe a conservative without calling them names.

The Answer is:
TRUMPway - Doing things differently than other presidents and getting more done.

You are a liberal if you think losing elections gives you a mandate.

You are a liberal if you like celebrities unless they are Republicans.

 You are a liberal if the Alaska wilderness is more important than national security or our economic independence from foreign oil.

You are a liberal if you think Jim Bakker is a crook.

You are a liberal if you think terror threats are merely a nuisance.

The Answer is:
TRUMPtweet - Communicating with
the American people instead of
having the media spin his comments.

You are a liberal if you agree with leaders of ungrateful nations that have been liberated by the United States.

You are a liberal if the Clinton Presidential Library is a place you want to visit.

You are a liberal if you can dish it out but can't take it.

You are a liberal if you don't understand conservative viewpoints.

You are a liberal if you build walls around yourself.

The Answer is:
TRUMPgreat - The author of
Making America Great Again.

You are a liberal if you think Donovan McNabb is a great quarterback, and you are a member of the press in Philadelphia.

You are a liberal if you think the President of the United States should let reporters be rude when asking questions.

 You are a liberal if you think conservatives are opposite of liberals.

You are a liberal if you don't believe in or want personal property rights.

You are a liberal if you are a bigot.

The Answer is:
TRUMPunity - Standing by our president, regardless of the lies being told by the press.

You are a liberal if you think all women are feminists.

You are a liberal if you want to oppress people.

You are a liberal if you think Republicans are in office only for big business.

You are a liberal if you liked the phrase that promoted 'never-trump'.

You are a liberal if you think the results need to be challenged when a Republican is elected.

You are a liberal if you want freedom for all religions, except Christianity.

The Answer is:
TRUMPhuge - The biggest election upset in American politics.

You are a liberal if you trust the government.

You are a liberal if the outcome of elections dictates your happiness.

You are a liberal if you want  Christians to be quiet.

You are a liberal if you want the Jewish people to give the land of Israel away to other nations.

You are a liberal if you are part of the swamp fighting against Donald Trump.

You are a liberal if you believe that you are in control.

The Answer is:
TRUMPquality - Doing the job the right way and not letting politics dictate how to do it.

You are a liberal if you think that only good people are Democrats.

You are a liberal if you don't know what the word IS means.

 You are a liberal if you want to take the fun out of life.

You are a liberal if you are going to try and make me look like a liberal.

You are a liberal if you make a joke and then state legal disclaimers so you won't get sued.

You are a liberal if you are going to try and sue anybody you can.

The Answer is:
TRUMPfirst - Putting America first over his own interests.

You are a liberal if you are a crook.

You are a liberal if you have other people speak for you.

You are a liberal if you don't like big business.

You are a liberal if you think Bill O'Reily isn't looking out for you.

You are a liberal if you think that this country is headed in the wrong direction only when a Republican is the president.

 You are a liberal if you want to rename your city police officers "hospitality attendants."

The Answer is:
TRUMPempire - Making lots of money, then using his own money to run for president.

You are a liberal if you think that morality is defined by rules.

You are a liberal if you have a litmus test for judges.

You are a liberal if you want your test results or polls to be taken seriously but don't want the results of your test scrutinized.

You are a liberal if you think that any test is an accurate result of knowledge.

You are a liberal if you're a hater.

The Answer is:
TRUMPery - Being several steps ahead of the Trump haters, including the media.

You are a liberal if you think bad news for the country is good news for you.

You are a liberal if you think that we are not a decent country.

 You are a liberal if you think you and your friends represent minorities' best interests.

You are a liberal if you purposely disguise your true intentions with words that sound good.

You are a liberal if you think Republicans are heartless, unsophisticated and ruthless.

The Answer is:
TRUMParty - An 8 year celebration,
bringing family values back to the
country.

You are a liberal if you want to disagree with my opinion being expressed.

You are a liberal if you think conservatives are irrational.

You are a liberal if you don't understand that Donald Trump is a pragmatist.

You are a liberal if you think conservatives make blanket statements.

You are a liberal if you think the glass is half empty.

You are a liberal if you think tax dollars need to be spent on promoting sex among elementary students.

The Answer is:
TRUMPsavior - Saving our country from the liberals and politics as usual.

You are a liberal if votes need to be recounted if a Democrat lost.

You are a liberal if you don't want people to say Merry Christmas.

You are a liberal if you think liberalism doesn't need faith.

You are a liberal if you think Thanksgiving is just a holiday to have some days off.

Thanksgiving Day

You are a liberal if you don't think that God has anything to do with the American culture.

The Answer is:
TRUMPtopia - The apex where the best is reached for the majority of
citizens.

You are a liberal if you think conservatives are intolerant people.

You are a liberal if you think the Declaration of Independence is not a historical document.

You are a liberal if you think the Constitution of the United States needs all the statements about a Creator taken out of the document.

Join US..
..for a
devil
of a good
time!

You are a liberal if you only like Democrats.

You are a liberal if you think people are the problem.

The Answer is:
TRUMPkin - Policies that are improving the standard of living for all.

You are a liberal if you think tax dollars need to be spent on the arts.

You are a liberal if you call Indians, Native Americans because it's politically correct.

You are a liberal if you want your opinion expressed but don't want people to know who you are.

You are a liberal if you think your message isn't being heard by the American people.

You are a liberal if you think someone makes too much money.

The Answer is:
TRUMPgiving - The approach of thinking about others first.

You are a liberal if you think Oliver North doesn't know which group of people fight for liberty.

You are a liberal if you decide you know what someone is like without listening or reading more about them.

You are a liberal if you think Donald Trump is not the president of the United States.

You are a liberal if you think Republicans have talking points.

You are a liberal if you try to please everybody you get to know.

The Answer is:
TRUMPmas - The time of year when everyone gets together to celebrate the birth of a new way to lead the country to new heights.

You are a liberal if you think Donald Trump was a mistake.

You are a liberal if you look to focus groups or polls to help you decide what direction to take.

You are a liberal if you believe that the social security administration is putting money aside for you from your paycheck.

You are a liberal if certain mascots of sports teams represent characters and names that are offensive and need to be changed.

The Answer is:
TRUMPlicans - The crowds
that show up at every rally with
President Trump.

 You are a liberal if peace on Earth comes when the military leaves.

You are a liberal if you think Neal Boortz doesn't understand the flat tax plan.

You are a liberal if you look to the government for help.

You are a liberal if a judge can't be appointed because he may be a conservative.

You are a liberal if you believe terrorists are innocent and covered under the Geneva Convention.

You are a liberal if you blame others.

The Answer is:
EL-TRUMPO - The Rush Limbaugh
of politics

You are a liberal if you think that a Hispanic American can't be a Republican.

You are a liberal if you believe that a Black American can't be a Republican.

You are a liberal if you think that women can't be Republicans.

 You are a liberal if you think that water-efficient toilets save water. (How many times do you flush now?)

You are a liberal if you think Laura Ingraham is a dumb blonde.

The Answer is:
TRUMPhouse - Making
where we live a home,
safe and secure.

You are a liberal if you think that Democrats work with Republicans, but Republicans don't want to work with Democrats.

You are a liberal if you think the American people are not generous.

You are a liberal if you can't decide whether popular vote or the electoral college should determine the outcome of the U.S. presidential election.

You are a liberal if you think daytime TV is good entertainment.

You are a liberal if the problem is the Church.

The Answer is:
TRUMPeconomy - Record stock market highs, lowest unemployment ever.

 You are a liberal if you think Easter is about candy and rabbits.

You are a liberal if you think chivalry should be dead.

You are a liberal if you think that the United Nations 'Oil for Food' program was a success.

You are a liberal if you think God is an election tool and not your Savior.

You are a liberal if you think that Glenn Beck doesn't have a sense of humor.

You are a liberal if the right is wrong.

The Answer is:
TRUMPbase - Bringing
more people in to the
Republican party.

 You are a liberal if you don't believe that law enforcement officials are in place for your safety.

You are a liberal if you call yourself a red state Democrat.

You are a liberal if you call yourself a fiscal conservative but a social moderate.

You are a liberal if you are wearing a blue bracelet.

You are a liberal if you don't use the term 'president' when they are Republicans.

You are a liberal if illegal immigrants should be allowed to vote.

The Answer is:
TRUMPcentury - The lasting effect that will be felt in this country for years to come.

You are a liberal if you think illegal immigrants should be let into the country.

You are a liberal if you kneel during the national anthem to protest police brutality.

You are a liberal if you kneel during the national anthem because you think the country is racist.

You are a liberal if 5.5 billion tax cut reform bill is considered crumbs for the American people.

The Answer is:
TRUMPchampion - The
final knock out punch to
the Democrat party.

You are a liberal if you want to keep the Obamacare Mandate.

You are a liberal if you don't think the GDP (Gross Domestic Product) will ever get above 3 percent again.

You are a liberal if the creation of over 7 million jobs only happens when a Democrat is president.

You are a liberal if unemployment being the lowest in history had nothing to do with President Trump.

You are a liberal if the coal and steel industries should be shut down.

The Answer is:
TRUMPbreed - A movement in politics that only comes once in a lifetime.

You are a liberal if the Dow Jones reaching record highs because of Republicans is a myth.

You are a liberal if the rebound of economic confidence being over a 17 year high is the result of a Democrat administration.

You are a liberal if cutting regulations doesn't save over 8 billion dollars.

You are a liberal if withdrawing from the Paris Climate Agreement is going to make the environment worse.

You are a liberal if a government shut down is bad for the country.

The Answer is:
TRUMPface - The shock
on liberal faces when
Trump keeps winning.

You are a liberal if you think that mass shootings are done by people that vote Republican.

You are a liberal if the North American Free Trade Agreement was fair for the U.S.

 You are a liberal if companies like Toyota, Mazda, Broadcom Limited and Foxconn deciding to build plants in America had nothing to do with President Donald Trump.

You are a liberal if you care more for illegal immigrants then U.S. citizens.

The Answer is:
TRUMPfriends - Anybody with a
Trump hat or Trump shirt.

You are a liberal if you think the USA should be friends with Communist Cuba.

You are a liberal if socialism should be taught at every school.

You are a liberal if you think the Trans-Pacific Partnership was good for America.

You are a liberal if you think the #walkaway movement is just a fad.

You are a liberal if you think other countries don't want President Trump to visit them.

The Answer is:
TRUMPmusic - God
Bless the USA

You are a liberal if the increase in the median household income is reported as bad news when a Republican is president.

 You are a liberal if poverty being the lowest level ever recorded only happens when a Democrat is president.

You are a liberal if you are tired of all the politics going on, but don't realize that President Trump is the one ending politics as the status quo.

You are a liberal if money is your god.

The Answer is:
TRUMPsuper - Leading the
entire world into peace.

You are a liberal if you say good things about Republicans after they die, but not when they were alive.

You are a liberal if you think abortion is OK even up to birth.

You are a liberal if a wall on our border is bad for the country.

You are a liberal if certain Christmas songs offend you and the radio station should stop playing them.

You are a liberal when President Trump says the same thing Democrat presidents have said and you disagree with him because you hate Trump.

The Answer is:
TRUMPhero - Beating the competition, with one hand tied behind his back.

You are a liberal if you think Republicans have a mental disorder.

You are a liberal if you think entertainers, athletes and politicians are more important then the police or daily workers.

 You are a liberal if you think masculinity is toxic.

You are a liberal if you think Robert Muller needs more time to find evidence that President Trump is a crook.

You are a liberal if you think conservatives are wanting to destroy this country.

The Answer is:
TRUMPwinner- Never
getting tired of winning.

You are a liberal if you hassle or beat people up because they are wearing a Make America Great hat.

You are a liberal if you think a strong America hurts other countries.

You are a liberal if you trust the Democrat party.

You are a liberal if you want this country to become socialist.

You are a liberal if you think trees have heart beats.

You are a liberal if you want to ban plastic straws.

The Answer is:
TRUMPoline - Jumping for
joy every time Trump talks.

You are a liberal if you believe that the shadow government trying to get President Trump out of office is good.

You are a liberal if you think President Trump is the source of Fake News.

You are a liberal if you don't know what Trump Derangement Syndrome is or that you have it.

You are a liberal if you think Donald Trump destroyed the Republican party.

You are a liberal if you think that our trade deals with other countries are fair.

The Answer is:
TRUMPosium - A gathering
of like minded Americans.

You are a liberal if you think putting tariffs on other countries is hurting the USA.

You are a liberal if you don't see that the Democrat party is becoming obsolete because of Donald Trump.

You are a liberal if you think Donald Trump is a politician.

 You are a liberal if you believe that President Trump has ruined the planet.

You are a liberal if you think President Obama made racial relationships better in the country.

The Answer is:
TRUMPalize - The last thing needed to finalize our country's move to greatness.

You are a liberal if you don't know how or why Donald Trump was elected.

You are a liberal if you don't recognize good news for America and the citizens.

You are a liberal if you think Donald Trump should be impeached.

You are a liberal if you don't know that the vote against impeachment in the house of representative of President Trump was bipartisan.

You are a liberal if you are a snowflake.

The Answer is:
TRUMPiness - A good feeling
you get when talking about
Donald Trump.

You are a liberal if you think the Betsy Ross Flag is racist.

You are a liberal if you think the money President Obama sent to Iran was not American tax dollars.

You are a liberal if you think President Trump has nothing to do with over 7 million new jobs.

You are a liberal if you don't want people to have a good time.

You are a liberal if you think the Democrats and the media don't work together to promote lies about Trump.

The Answer is:
TRUMPhobia - The fear that President Trump is the best president ever.

You are a liberal if you don't realize that the true party of compassion is the Republicans.

You are a liberal if you think America should feel guilty for being the best country in the world.

 You are a liberal if you think President Trump did not sign a trade deal with China.

You are a liberal if you don't know what Operation Chaos is about.

You are a liberal if you don't know that conservatives love America and the culture.

The Answer is:
TRUMPDiplomacy - Saying what needs to be said to foreign countries.

You are a liberal if you don't believe that conservatives love people.

You are a liberal if you don't know that President Trump has done more for the middle class, than any other president.

You are a liberal if you don't know that President Trump has done more for the economy, than any other president.

 You are a liberal if you don't know that President Trump has done more for jobs, than any other president.

You are a liberal if you coddle the lazy.

The Answer is:
TRUMPPhilosophy - That
America is a force of good in
the world, and we back it up.

You are a liberal if you don't know that President Trump has done more for higher wages, than any other president.

 You are a liberal if you don't know that President Trump has done more for Israel, than any other president.

You are a liberal if you don't know that President Trump has done more for reducing illegal immigration, than any other president.

You are a liberal if you don't know that President Trump has done more to solve America's trade deficit, than any other president.

The Answer is:
TRUMPLivingLarge - In the process of getting all Americans more money to live larger.

You are a liberal if you don't know that President Trump has achieved more than any other president.

 You are a liberal if you don't know that President Trump has exposed politics as usual.

You are a liberal if President Trump is just an actor to you.

You are a liberal if you only hear negative things from President Trump.

You are a liberal if you don't hear President Trump saying positive things.

You are a liberal if you don't know that President Trump promotes goodness.

The Answer is:
TRUMPian - A believer in the policies of President Trump.

You are a liberal if you don't realize President Trump is too legit to quit.

You are a liberal if you like voter fraud.

You are a liberal if you vote opposite of your faith.

You are a liberal if you think Donald Trump doesn't know where Ukraine is located.

You are a liberal if you are against closed borders.

You are a liberal if English should not be the primary language of the United States.

The Answer is:
TRUMPite - A person that will vote for President Trump, but not put a bumper sticker on their car.

You are a liberal if you don't want mandatory drug screening before getting welfare.

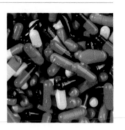

You are a liberal if giving money to illegals is OK, but not to our veterans that sacrificed for this country.

You are a liberal if you want boys to compete in girl sports.

You are a liberal you think Article 2 allows the president to do anything he wants.

You are a liberal if you think Trump wants to be king.

The Answer is:
TRUMPfighter - Someone that stands up to liberals and tells them the truth.

You are a liberal if you think the election is the coronation of Trump.

You are a liberal if you don't know about joy.

You are a liberal if you call your pets companions, because its more dignified.

You are a liberal if you don't think that Donald Trump is a president of the people, for the people and by the people.

You are a liberal if you are looking for solutions to problems that President Trump already solved.

The Answer is:
TRUMPified - Once a Democrat, now a Republican.

You are a liberal if you want President Trump to just go away.

You are a liberal if the media is your religion.

You are a liberal if the media is your gospel.

You are a liberal if the media is your god.

You are a liberal if you call President Trump #klanpresident.

You are a liberal if you think President Trump was not pro-active dealing with COVID-19.

You are a liberal if Trump makes you cry.

The Answer is:
TRUMPoracle - The top kahuna,
becoming the leader with hard work
and fortitude to get the job done.

You are a liberal if you don't know that Blexit is growing.

You are a liberal if you don't know that Jexit is growing.

You are a liberal if you don't know that Lexit is growing.

You are a liberal if you try and make money off a crisis.

You are a liberal if you follow the FAKE News on CNN, ABC, NBC, CBS, MSNBC, and FOX.

You are a liberal if you aren't aware that President Trump is the only one NOT playing politics.

The Answer is:
TRUMPreal - Genuine concern to make The United States the best in the world.

You are a liberal if President Trump's confidence bothers you.

You are a liberal if President Trump's language bothers you.

You are a liberal if you think Jeffrey Epstein killed himself.

You are a liberal if you want this country to fail under President Trump.

You are a liberal if you think a corporation exists to provide jobs.

You are a liberal if you want President Trump to stop tweeting.

Contact - johnbushman1@outlook.com

The Answer is:
TRUMPgold - Highly sought after
and precious.

God Bless our Troops.

The Answer is:
TRUMPunique - One of a kind,
once in a lifetime, the best is yet
to come.

Index

Trump Commandments
1. We are the best country in the World.

Trump Commandments
2. Thou shall put America First.

Trump Commandments
3. Thou shall not have any other countries before thee.

Trump Commandments
4. Thou shall not curse the USA.

Trump Commandments
5. Remember what makes us great and keep it in focus.

Trump Commandments
6. Honor the founders and the constitution.

Trump Commandments
7. Thou shall not kill the unborn.

Trump Commandments
8. Thou shall not commit high
treason against the USA.

Trump Commandments
9. Thou shall not steal from America and give to other countries.

Trump Commandments
10. Thou shall not covet other peoples money.

Trump Commandments
11. Thou shall create fair trade.

Trump Commandments
12. Thou shall build a wall.

Trump Commandments
13. Thou shall cut taxes.

Trump Commandments
14. Thou shall bring jobs back to America.

Trump Commandments
15. Thou shall enact deregulations.

Trump Commandments
16. Thou shall grow the economy.

Trump Commandments
17. Thou shall expose
establishment politicians.

Trump Commandments
18. Thou shall destroy terrorist networks around the world.

Trump Commandments
19. Thou shall achieve energy independence.

Trump Commandments
20. Thou shall rebuild the military.